THE
SILK
ROAD
.

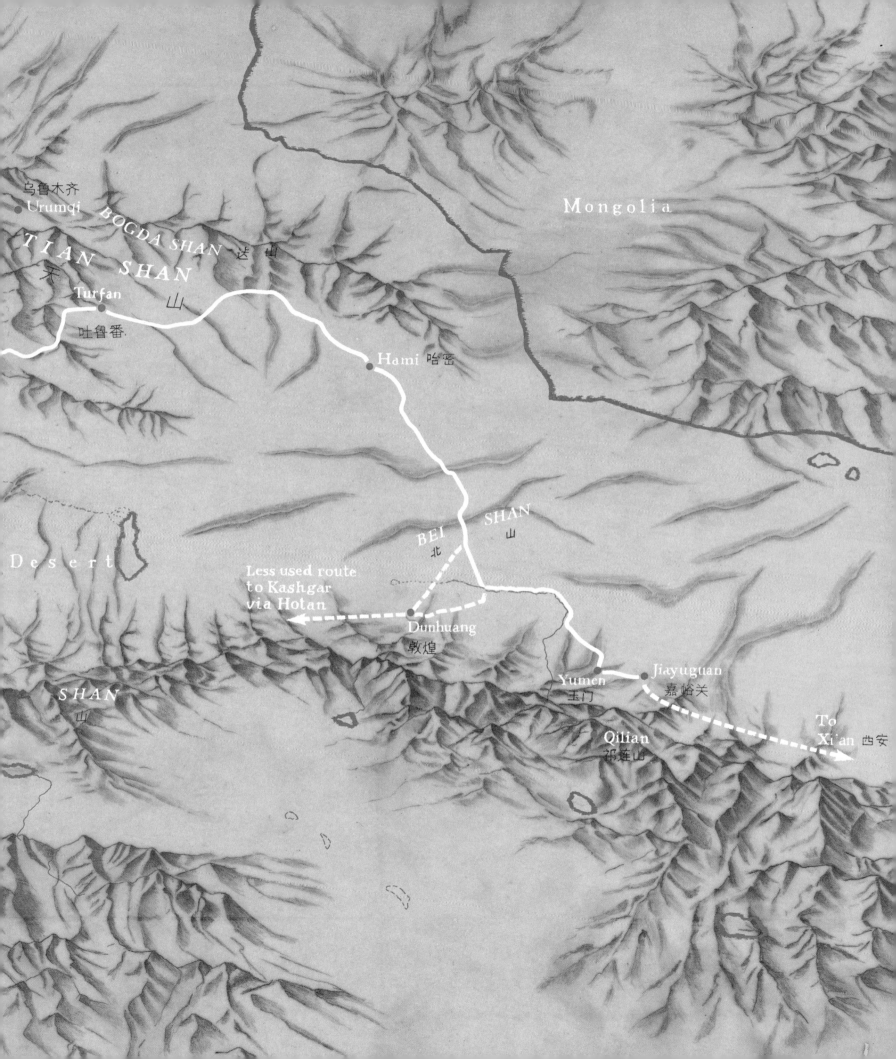

BEYOND THE CELESTIAL KINGDOM

THE
SILK ROAD

COLIN THUBRON

PHOTOGRAPHS BY
CARLOS NAVAJAS

SIMON AND SCHUSTER
New York   London   Toronto   Sydney   Tokyo

SIMON AND SCHUSTER

Simon & Schuster Building
Rockefeller Center
1230 Avenue of the Americas
New York, New York 10020

First published in 1989 in Great Britain
by Pyramid Books, an imprint of
The Hamlyn Publishing Group Limited
a division of The Octopus Publishing Group,
Michelin House, 81 Fulham Road, London SW3 6RB

Printed in Spain by Cayfosa

1 3 5 7 9 10 8 6 4 2

Library of Congress Catalog Card Number:
89-21809

ISBN 0-671-70175-4

PAGE ONE: Xi'an.
PAGE TWO: The Apak Hoja mausoleum, Kashgar.

CONTENTS

PART ONE

WHERE
CHINA DIES

WHERE CHINA DIES

Decorated door at Jiayuguan Fort, built to defend the Qilian Mountains to the South and the Black Mountains to the North. Jiayuguan, meaning 'Barrier of the Pleasant Valley', is situated on one of the earliest parts of the Great Wall.
PREVIOUS PAGE Jiayuguan Fort.

If a traveller were to seek out on the map the most landlocked spot in Asia, the arms of his compasses would intersect deep in the Chinese province of Sinkiang — a mountain-circled wilderness whose heart is pure desert. The geological thrust of the Himalayas to the south — they are still rising at the rate of six inches a year — has deprived this whole region of monsoon rains, and all but one of the snow-fed rivers evaporate before they find a sea. Here, where the Silk Road once started on its five-thousand-mile course to the Mediterranean — the forests have thinned and died within historical memory.

Here too, traditional China petered out. The Chinese, who grew up along the great eastern rivers, feared wilderness and despised nomadism. Within their Great Wall, they believed, spread all true civilisation — the order and harmony of the Celestial Kingdom, ruled by the Son of Heaven. Beyond was only a barbarian dark, haunted by robbers and drifting herdsmen of inexplicable habits. Those Chinese who died there would be torn from their desert graves by demons, and Buddhists be condemned for ever to lowly reincarnations. Even today Chinese talk of those travelling west through the Great Wall as going 'outside the mouth' — beyond the pale.

Ming fort of Jiayuguan

The site of this 'mouth' is the great Ming fort of Jiayuguan, wrapped round by the last of the Great Wall, which finds its end nearby in a grey-blue precipice. It is a bitter, windbeaten bastion thrust into the desert beyond a nondescript steel town, and the tunnel through its western gate was once covered with despairing messages and poems, scratched on the brick by exiles as they departed into the unknown.

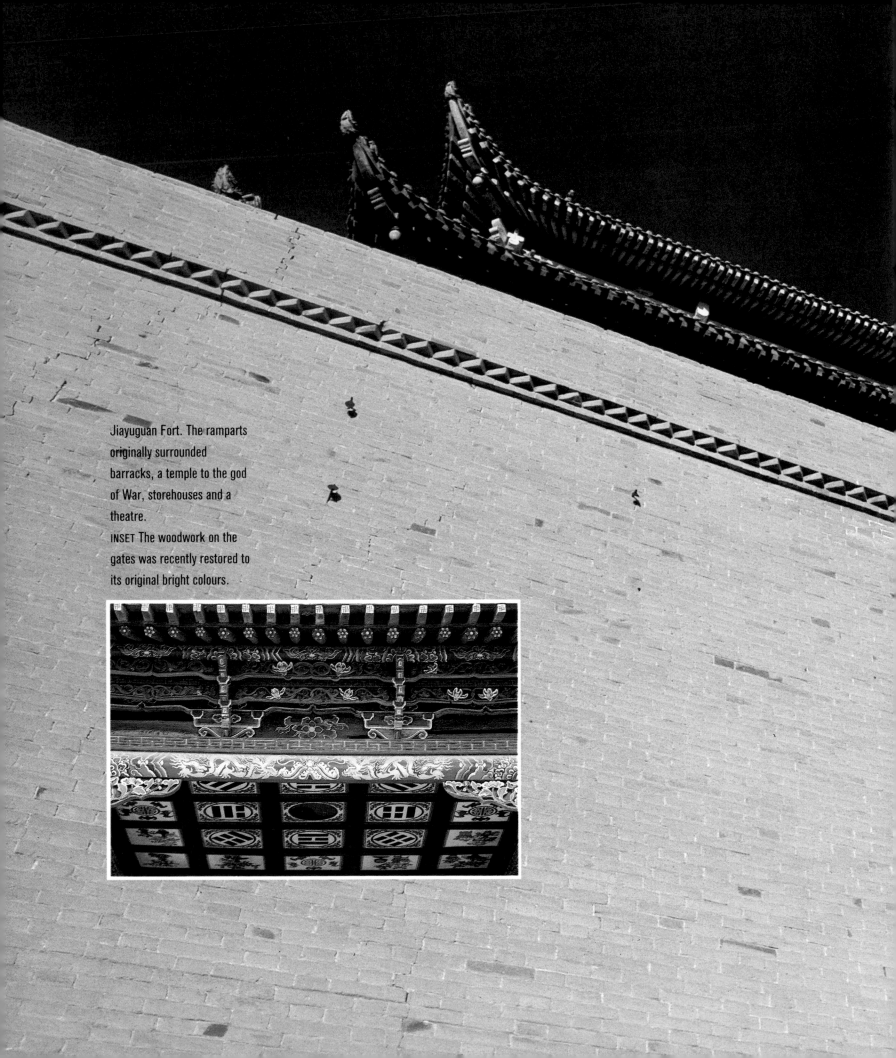

Jiayuguan Fort. The ramparts
originally surrounded
barracks, a temple to the god
of War, storehouses and a
theatre.
INSET The woodwork on the
gates was recently restored to
its original bright colours.

One of the gates of Jiayuguan Fort, its curving roofs outlined at sunset. The wooden columns, INSET, are painted red and rise into intricately carved and decorated capitals.

The 'Sand City'

From Jiayuguan the Silk Road passes west to Dunhuang, the 'Sand City' of Marco Polo, which in fact he scarcely mentioned. Already, in his day, the great cities of this area were vanishing into the sand, and nowadays the drive to Dunhuang takes you across deepening desert. On many days extended mirages hover all along the horizon — lakes and rivers misted in their own reflections, while the ghosts of water-logged trees and houses shimmer beyond.

Buddhist shrines near Dunhuang

The Buddhist shrines near Dunhuang have become a tourist centre almost overnight. A triple tier of concrete galleries, scaffolds their frescoed caves, which are mostly kept shut by dilapidation and the lack of caretakers. But the richness and variety of those shrines which are open assail you almost unbearably. As you scrutinise them in near-darkness, a double sense of ignorance and satiety subsumes you. Between one cave and another you leapfrog centuries. Half-naked Hindu figures parade along walls fourteen hundred years old. From their vermillion faces, oxidised to black, the white eyes glare fantastically out. In other caves giant Tang Buddhas sit inert and undamaged in their multi-ringed haloes and mandorlas. Still other murals have faded to shadowy comic-strips.

There is something moving and desolate now about these ancient certainties — the frescoed Buddhas and Bodhisattvas reproduced over and over, as if repetition made them true. But the monks who once thronged here have all gone, and so has their quietude.

From here the Silk Road bifurcates. In times of unrest, the caravans would move south through the sparse towns along the foot of the Kunlum Mountains, protected from robbers by the Taklimakan desert. But more often they would brave the great northern route with its line of rich oases — Turfan, Korla, Kuqa, Aksu — and hope to evade marauders from the grasslands just to the north.

ABOVE AND LEFT Decorated panels at Jiayuguan Fort. Foreign merchants often waited here for months at a time for permission to pass on eastwards into China along the Silk Road.

The walls of Jiayuguan Fort: 35 feet high, with a circumference of over 3,000 feet. According to local legend, the fortifications were so meticulously planned that only one brick remained unused at the end of construction.

Turfan and the Flame Mountains

ABOVE Of the original buildings at Jiayuguan, there only remain the gates, the theatre and the temple, which has been converted into a museum.
RIGHT Ornate capitals, rising to the roof's distinctive curves.

Turfan is the largest and strangest of these places — a town spread on gravel-strewn plains which drop to the deepest waterless depression on earth. In summer it is so hot here that you can boil an egg by burying it in the sand. In winter it is the coldest region in China. Yet as you approach Turfan over the plain, the divide between desert and sown is brilliant and sudden. In this rainless land, the grain-bearing fields and the orchards are threaded by channels of cold water which emerge enigmatically from the ground.

You wander the suburbs in astonishment. They are idly beautiful. In autumn the courtyard trellises sag with grapes, and a plethora of lemons and apricots appears.

This fertility is spread by more than four hundred subterranean water-courses, which have been burrowed like horizontal wells, sometimes ten miles long, from underground springs in the nearby Flame Mountains. Precisely when this ingenious irrigation arrived here is unknown, but its technology came, almost certainly, from ancient Persia — a sign that the Silk Road had moved out of classical China into the complex flow of Central Asia. You may still enter these tunnels through a whining veil of flies and blunder for hundreds of yards under the desert, while your torchlight wobbles uncertainly over the soft earth walls and the water runs cold at your knees.

18

The 460 Mogao Caves in the Mingsha Hills, south-east of Dunhuang, are the world's richest source of Buddhist art. Frescos and stucco sculptures date from about 220 AD and depict religious subjects as well as local patrons who financed the excavation of the caves.

Camels near Dunhuang. According to the Chinese chronicle, Pei Shih, desert camels are sensitive to the approach of sandstorms: 'When such a wind is about to arrive, only the old camels have advance knowledge of it, and they bury their mouths in the sand. The men always take this as a sign, and they too immediately cover their noses and mouths by wrapping them in felt. This wind moves swiftly, and passes in a moment, and is gone, but if they did not so protect themselves, they would be in danger of sudden death.'

The sand dunes south of Mingsha are the most spectacular desert scenery on the Silk Road. The 820-foot Mingsha dune rises steeply and overlooks Crescent Lake — visitors can make the ascent by camel or on foot.

The Oasis Dwellers

The oasis-dwellers, you later notice, are different from the native Chinese. They are burlier. Their eyes glitter wider, in round faces. They talk and gesture with an easy ebullience the women move in violently-coloured dresses, and their ears drop bright pendants. The men show a Levantine swagger and astuteness.

These are Uighur — a Moslem people of Turkic origin who abandoned nomadism in the twelfth century and settled the oases. It was they and people like them — Uzbeks, Kazaks, Kirgiz — who occupied the heart of the Silk Road: a lost Turkic nation which never united. Hardy traders and opportunists, the Uighur led their camel and donkey caravans from well to brackish well and dealt in horses, cloth, jade, spices, tea and a miasma of local products. 'These people,' ran a ninth-century inscription, 'who were known to drink blood like savages, have turned to eating the crops of the earth.'

Of the sparse fourteen million inhabitants of Sinkiang — a province comprising one sixth of all China — some six million are Uighur. But westward migration has swelled the native Chinese to almost equal numbers, creating ugly, periodic riots. For the two people are deeply unlike. Where the Chinese are conventional, bureaucratic and collective, the Uighur are relaxed, sensuous and individualistic. They love dancing (which Confucius thought ridiculous) and cherish their music and horses.

Gaochang

The evidence of this historical pendulum — of Chinese domination and Uighur independence — is all around. Dead cities fringe the oases in a mud ruin of battlements and palaces — cities which were founded by the Chinese but reverted to self-rule as the imperial power faded. Built of compacted earth and brick, they rise huge above their plains — wind-blurred shapes, from which all decoration has been rubbed away. At Gaochang, in particular, a tenth-century Uighur capital, the classical Chinese plan shines through a jumble of later building: outer and inner cities, palace compounds, a vestige of grid-pattern streets. More than four miles of ramparts circle it, lifting to thirty feet, but the labyrinth of walls inside discloses a strange, Plasticine city, smooth and yellow as the soil from which it rises. Your feet crunch and rasp over the compacted earth; here and there the walls break into chunks and cones and spires, and you imagine you are wandering a Cappadocian valley. Yet the feel is of a place standing midstream between East and West. There are stupas, Persian-style tombs, the ruins of Christian and Manichean monasteries; and the style of the Buddhist sculptures discovered here — heads whose features disturbingly suggest Apollo's — has been ascribed to the influence of Alexander the Great.

The stupendousness of these abandoned cities, which withered away with the Silk Road, touches all Sinkiang with the sadness of redundancy. Today the route's traffic has dwindled to a trickle of trucks and lorries, mostly carrying coal and timber. The borders with the Soviet Union and Pakistan have opened tentatively, allowing a little silk, cotton, tea and tobacco to leave in exchange for vehicles and electrical goods. But the old ways — the camel trains, the caravanserais — have finished within living memory. □

BELOW A sculpture in the Mogao Caves. As the stone in these caves is soft and sandy, these sculptures were moulded on wood frames. LEFT Pagoda in a paddy field outside Dunhuang.

Gobi Desert sandscape on the
way to Turfan, once known
as 'Storehouse of Wind': the
distinctive noise of wind
roaring over the dunes was
referred to by Marco Polo as
'rumbling sands'.

ABOVE Child's bed in Kashgar.
LEFT The colourful *dopa*, or
embroidered cap, is worn by
the Uighur people. Women
may also wear veils or scarves.
RIGHT Children in Turfan.

RIGHT Scene at Turfan
market, where cloth, hats,
embroidery and clothing is
sold, along with carpets and
fruit and vegetables.
BELOW Wheat for bread is
grown round Turfan, as are
maize, cotton, grapes and
vegetables.

Views of the Suleiman mosque
and minaret, also called the
Emin minaret. Made of
unglazed mudbricks in the
Afghan style, the minaret is
one of the Silk Road's most
striking architectural features.

The Emin minaret, which was commissioned by Emin Hoja in 1777, and designed by a Uighur architect named Ibrahim. The mosque has a beamed ceiling supported by wooden pillars, and a domed roof.

The Flaming Mountains, north-
east of Turfan. Wind erosion
has uncovered unusually red
clay in parts of the hills, so
that when the sun catches
them, they appear to be on
fire. Moreover, the hills absorb
the sun's rays, creating
extremely hot temperatures.

The Buddhist cave centre at Bezeklik in the Flaming Mountains, carved out between the fifth and fourteenth centuries. Frescos and life-sized painted stucco Buddhas were discovered when the caves were excavated early this century.

The ruins of Gaochang, a provincial capital in the sixth and seventh centuries which would have housed some 50,000 people. Archaeologists discovered fine mosaics, statues, manuscripts and wall paintings here.

ABOVE The ruined city of Jiaohe, set on an island between two rivers. The remains date from the Tang Dynasty (618-907).

Landscape near Jiaohe.
ABOVE The Buddhist cave
centre at Bezeklik, carved out
between the fifth and
fourteenth centuries. Frescos
and life-sized painted stucco
Buddhas were discovered
when the caves were
excavated early this century.

The ancient city of Jiaohe
flourished at the same period
as Gaochang, and was also a
provincial capital for a time.
The remains of mudbrick
houses, temples and watch-
towers can still be seen.

Views of the red sandstone
hills of the Flaming Mountains,
much featured in local legend
and also in the sixteenth-
century Chinese novel, *Journey
to the West* by Wu Cheng'en

Countryside around Jiaohe.
Marco Polo said of this region:
'The land produces grain and
excellent wine. But in winter,
the cold is more intense than
is known in any other part of
the land.'

LEFT Man at work in the
vineyards at Turfan: the
seedless grapes from here
are famous throughout China,
and most houses have a
grape-drying room.
ABOVE Bundles of rope for
sale.

A Kazak mother and her child in their yurt (a traditional felt covered circular tent) in Nanshan. The Kazaks are semi-nomadic but have been loosely organised into communes by the state.

PART TWO

HEAVENLY
MOUNTAINS

HEAVENLY MOUNTAINS

The Chinese historian Ma Twan-lin described the Gobi Desert as 'nothing in any direction but the sky and the sands, travellers find nothing to guide them but the bones of men and beasts and the droppings of camels'.
PREVIOUS PAGE The Tian Shan Heavenly Mountains.

A ninety-eight-year-old merchant sits pampered among his sons. His face's skin has wizened over its bones, but the eyes shine shrewd and the cheeks are still nested in a thick beard. 'In the old days I used to lead a caravan from Turfan to Kashgar,' he says. 'It was hard going — 65 days of travel. We'd set out in March, perhaps, and start back again in October — another two months — bringing back silk cocoons to Turfan.'
'And the profit?'
'From that one trip I could feed my family of nine.' His sons nod and smile. 'But that's all over. Nobody does that any more. I made my last journey more than thirty years ago.'

Grasslands of the Kazaks

The Silk Road west is paved now, running from Turfan along the foot of the Tian Shan, the 'Heavenly Mountains', eight hundred miles to Kashgar. On one side the snow-peaks glitter clear of the haze; on the other the desert levels into the Taklimakan sands, glazed with stone and gravel washed down by floods. Through this schizophrenic landscape the tarmac highway links oases of wheat and orchards, where Chinese and Uighur cohabit uneasily, and the fields and poplar avenues, nourished by snowfed streams, sprawl over the sand.

If you turn north into the Tian Shan, the summer grasslands of the Kazaks lift about you with Alpine clarity. The streams are ice-rimmed even in April, and the people still cooped in their winter houses. They greet you curiously. Inside, stoves heat the walls through narrow vents, and you sit on a wooden platform covered with the thick felt rugs which the women weave. Outside, the yurt tents are trussed on timber platforms by the doors, waiting for the ascent to summer pastures. Proud in their shabby coats and fur-brimmed caps, the men sit with you — herdsmen of horses and cattle, with burnished Mongol cheekbones.

The Tian Shan Heavenly
Mountains, west of Turfan,
where Kazakh families graze
their cattle.
LEFT The 65-foot waterfall at
Baiyang Gou (White Poplar
Gully) in the Nan Shan
(Southern) mountains.

Landscape between Kuqa
and Aksu.
INSET A 'yurt', or felt tent
stretched over a frame of
sticks. In summer, Kazakh
families pitch them in the
foothills of the Celestial
Mountains.

Taklimakan

But turn off southward from the Silk Road, and you travel into wilderness. For miles an austere film of gravel camouflages the plain. In parts it is sprinkled with the cones of half-dead tamarisks; around their roots, flash-floods from the Tian Shan have swept thin all other soil, leaving the land carbuncled with thousands of tiny hillocks. As you penetrate deeper, you come upon a last village of wheat farmers perhaps, protected from true desert by the Tarim river and a belt of willows. But beyond this, after half a day's journey, you enter the terrible desert which the Uighur call Taklimakan, 'You go in and you never return.' It runs east-west for six hundred miles and is 250 miles wide — a wilderness of pure sand, whose dunes can reach to three hundred feet.

Almost all European explorers shunned it. Aurel Stein thought the Arabian deserts tame by comparison, and Sven Hedin called it 'the worst and most dangerous desert in the world'. Its black hurricane, the *kara-buran*, has buried whole caravans in a few hours, leaving their soldiers' bodies mummified in the sands.

The place is still said to be peopled by demons who lead travellers astray with hallucinatory noises. The sandstorms bring voices and ghosts, and sharp temperature changes set the high dunes into avalanche with a sound of drums. 'Sometimes the stray trader will hear as it were the tramp and hum of a great cavalcade of people away from the real line of march,' wrote Marco Polo, 'and taking this to be their own company they will follow the sound; and when day breaks they find that a cheat has been put on them and that they are in an ill plight. Even in daytime one hears those spirits talking. And sometimes you shall hear the sound of a variety of musical instruments . . .'

The dead vegetation and ruins which scatter the wastes suggest a river-flow once four times greater than it is now. Nothing else breaks the desolation. The only animal which can survive is the Bactrian camel, whose dinner-plate feet trot over the sand without sinking, and which starts to sweat — mildly — at a temperature in which a man would be dead.

Blacksmith at work in the oasis town of Kuqa. With its orchards and fields and colourful bazaars, travellers have always found Kuqa a pleasant resting place.

LEFT A jewellery workshop in Kuqa. On Fridays, the bazaar days, thousands of people from outlying areas throng the town in search of everything from harnesses to herbal remedies.

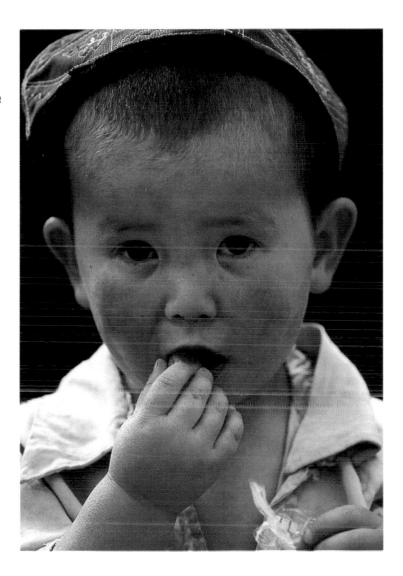

Kashgar

The Silk Road approaches the last great oasis, Kashgar, with scarcely a change in height. By the roadside the graves of Chinese labourers huddle in dusty mounds. Lured here in the Fifties by idealism or higher wages — or simply ordered out to settle this bitter province — these men died laying telegraph lines, building roads. Here and there, in homesickness, their graves have been laid facing east, back to the motherland.

But Kashgar is the least Chinese of China's cities. It belongs as much to legend as geography. Its history and inhabitants occupy some point where better-known events and people. Here was the nub of the 'great game' played by the Russians, British and Chinese for control of Central Asia, and at the turn of the century traders, archaeologists and spies mingled and interchanged in its inns and consulates. Its mud houses and painted balconies, the twisting lanes and bazaars, might belong to Shiraz or old Herat, rather than to the People's Republic. During the Cultural Revolution it suffered cruelly at the hands of Red Guards, as did the whole province, where seven thousand were killed; but now it has reverted to free trade and free workship, and its huge Sunday Market, on which more than fifty thousand people converge in their horse- and donkey-carts, suggests a resurgent Middle East.

The Southern Mountains, south of Urumqi. Melted snow from mountain tops was virtually the only source of water for travellers in this area of the Silk Road.
INSET Metalworkers in Kuqa.

Landscape between Kuqa and Aksu on the Silk Road. Woollen clothing, like the peasant woman's scarf, LEFT, is vital in winter. RIGHT The basic surroundings of a barber shop.

Kashgar Market

Architecture typical of Kuqa, a town where the old and new areas are divided by the ruins of the old city wall. The old part is highly atmospheric, with winding alleys and mudbrick walls.

They pour in from every part of the oasis and beyond. All morning the streets are jammed with scarlet-canopied horse taxis, carts carrying grain or wood, and tractor-drawn floats crowded with women, their brown veils thrown back.

But in the markets the pinched faces murmur and bargain in a quiet unknown to Arabia. Villagers sit all day by a few white radishes or a fiery heap of peppers and cumin, and seem unconcerned to sell. It is a familiar, Islamic world, where the wares are all grouped generically — in one corner an army of women squatting in the dust with the pigeons in netted baskets; in another a triple line of men selling skins, offal and goats' heads. And in the largest arena of all, the traders crowd together to form a man-made stadium where their horses are tested, and you can buy a young stallion or a cream-coloured camel for about a hundred pounds. Such bazaars are shunned by the native Chinese, who buy their wares in the clinical supermarkets. But the Chinese are still few in Kashgar. The slogans of the Cultural Revolution have been scrubbed away, and all that is visible from that era is an eighteen-metre granite statue of Mao Zedong — one of the last remaining public effigies of the Great Helmsman — who towers over the main street, lifting his hand to salute a future which went wrong. In a city of Moslems, who abhor any human image, his statue is a double insult, but a plan by the local authorities to blow it up only threatened the buildings nearby, and when they tried to saw it down they discovered it was reinforced with steel.

The heart of Kashgar is not there. It is at the city's Id Kah mosque whose courtyards fill on Fridays with the bowing and kneeling faithful. This, and the Apak Hoja mausoleum, burial-place of a seventeenth-century Moslem ruler of Kashgar, are the unspoken nerve-centres of the Uighur city.

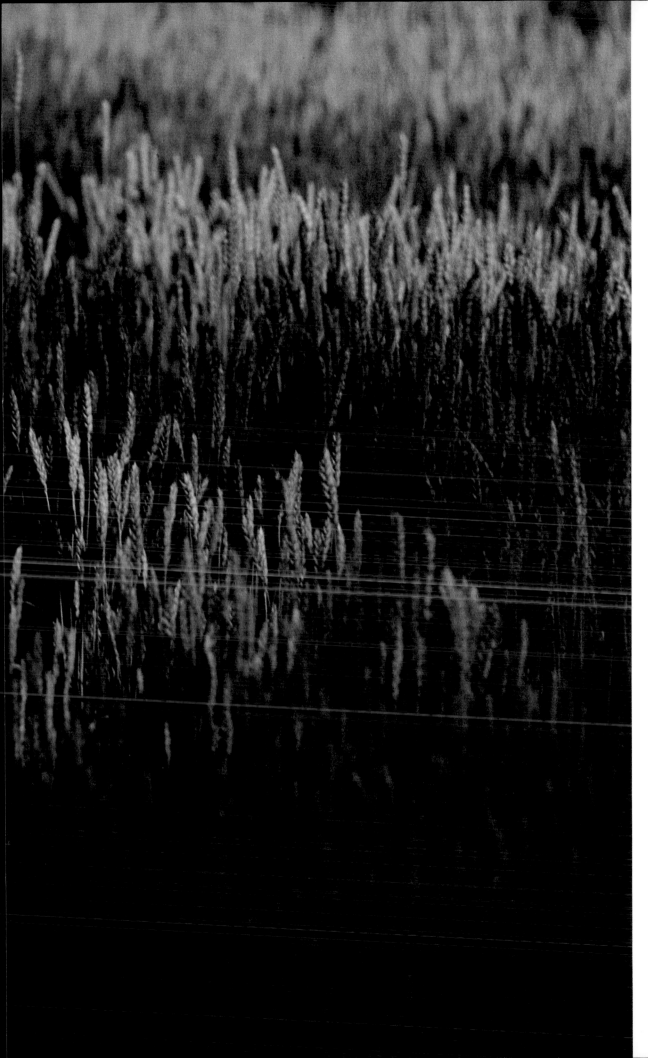

Aksu, where the Silk Road
crosses a tributary of the
Tarim river. One European
traveller said of the town:
'there are not many places
where the temples are more
wonderful or the gardens
of the rich Moslems
more beautiful.'

Mountain landscape in the
Taklimakan Desert, where the
Silk Road deteriorates into a
dusty track.
INSET Paved only in a few
area, the Road is now mainly
used by trucks. The drivers
sleep in the ditches either side
of the road.

Apak Hoja

The Apak Hoja is secluded: a green-tiled dome shining among poplars. Inside, some seventy catafalques mark the graves of the ruler and his descendants. The caretaker parrots their history in a stertorous shout, and avoids awkward questions: of the nearby tomb of Yakub Beg, the charismatic leader of a nineteenth-century Moslem rebellion against China, he says only that its stone was removed to make way for tree-planting.

Instead, officials concentrate on a smaller grave in the mausoleum — the tomb of a Uighur princess, who was sent as tribute to the emperor Qian Long. The emporer fell in love with her, it is said, but she repudiated his advances, and was forced by his mother to strangle herself. Later Qian Long was entombed beside her in the Qing dynasty mausolea near Beijing, but legend has returned her grave to Kashgar. The Chinese extol it as a symbol of their racial bonds with the Uighur. But the Uighur say it is a sign of Chinese cruelty, and pass the story like that to their children. □

Aksu: poplars are the most common trees to be found in the Gobi Desert oases. Aksu itself lies on the banks of the Aksu River, beneath a range of yellow loess cliffs.

Mountain scene in the
Taklimakan Desert, a region of
red-gold sand dunes 500 miles
long and 250 miles wide. Dead
stumps moulded into cones by
drifting sands are a common
feature of the landscape —
some as much as 50 feet high.

Scenes around the oasis
town of Kuqa.
ABOVE Donkey carts travel
from oasis to oasis selling
wood, which is used for
building, local crafts, and
firewood in winter.

RIGHT The prayerhall of the Aidkah Mosque, which dominates Kashgar's central square. The wooden ceiling is held up by 140 carved pillars painted green and on Friday afternoon prayers are often attended by as many as 10,000 people.

Kashgar Sunday Market, one of the largest in Central Asia.
ABOVE Bales of straw matting displayed for sale.
LEFT Horses, goats, sheep and camels are all available at the Market.

Scenes in the Sunday Market in Kashgar, east of the Tuman River.
FAR RIGHT Veiled Muslim women in the clothing section.
RIGHT A basket of boiled eggs, dyed red to distinguish them from the raw variety.

Herd of camels in the
Taklimakan Desert.
INSET Other than trucks
belonging to farming villages
or manufacturing enterprises,
traffic on the Silk Road
consists of bicycles, the
occasional motorcycle, and
horse- or donkey-drawn carts.

Views of the Aidkah Mosque in the heart of the old city. Built in 1442, this is the largest mosque in Kashgar, and worshippers come in truckloads from miles around.

Kashgar's trade links with Pakistan make its Sunday Market a huge attraction for peasants from all over the area. Here straw matting is displayed for sale.
LEFT Father and son hang out their wares.

The Sunday Market, the most important of the bazaars in Kashgar. Various attempts have been made to regulate the Market, but it remains a colourful and disorderly spectacle, thronged by thousands of people from miles around.

Like the suburban villages around it, Kashgar is largely a city of mudbrick, but wood is imported for minarets, balconies, supporting timbers and doors which are often ornately decorated.

The timber section of the
Sunday Market at Kashgar.
Trucks and carts carry small
amounts of wood from village
to village, but large quantities
would have to be bought here.

RIGHT Sacks of herbs for sale at the Sunday Market in Kashgar.
LEFT Women preparing food for sale in the Market: pilau rice, nan bread and mutton dumplings are all to be found here.

Behind a large graveyard
stands the Apak Hoja Tomb
at Kashgar: this perfectly
proportioned mausoleum has a
blue-and-gold tiled dome and
minarets at each corner ringed
with coloured tiles.

ABOVE Ornate columns in the mosque at the Apak Hoja Tomb in Kashgar.
LEFT The tiled façade of the Tomb, built in 1640.
RIGHT The ornate entrance is recessed into the façade of the Tomb.

Interior of the mosque adjacent to the Apak Hoja Tomb at Kashgar. Simple straw matting covering the floor contrasts with the heavily decorated pillars and capitals.

LEFT Interior of the mosque at the Apak Hoja Tomb, which is more recent than the mosque in the centre of Kashgar, and more ornate. There is also a religious school in the Tomb complex.

View of the interior of the domed Apak Hoja Tomb at Kashgar. Still used as a shrine, the room is about 25 metres square, and the tombs are draped in coloured saddle cloths.

Façade of the Apak Hoja Tomb, also known as the Tomb of the Fragrant Concubine, after a concubine who belonged to the Emperor Qianlong. According to legend, her body did not decompose, and remained 'fragrant'.
INSET An intricately carved gateway.

LEFT The graveyard opposite the Tomb of the Fragrant Concubine. In the care of one family for over a century, the necropolis is now looked after by the state.

PART THREE

Travelling
The Silk Road

TRAVELLING THE SILK ROAD

For more than two thousand years people have been crossing the ferocious mountains that lie between the Western world and China. Gemstones, precious spices but above all silk were transported along the route from China to Constantinople from as early as 200 BC. In its heyday during the Han Dynasty (206 BC to AD 220) great Bactrian camel trains would set out from the ancient Chinese capital at Xi'an, known as Sera Metropolis by the Western traders, on the first leg of their trading trek through the Haxi Corridor, in the shadow of the Qilian Shan, to the end of the Great Wall at Jiayuguan. Here, over a thousand years after the heyday of the Silk Road, the last great fort known as the 'Impregnable Pass Under Heaven' was constructed by General Feng Sheng in the Ming Dynasty. From Jiayuguan the road left the comparative safety of the Great Wall and the caravans started on their arduous, dangerous and incredibly slow progress around the northern rim of the Taklimakan Desert, or, in times of unrest they would make their way south following Marco Polo's route to Kashgar via Hotan. In the southern foothills of Tian Shan, 'The Heavenly Mountains', the camel trains would move with their escorts along the thin track that was 'The Road' past the oasis towns of Turfan, Korla, Kuqa, Aksu and on to Kashgar, which today lies near the Pakistan border.

From Kashgar some traders would take the western route over the Terek Pass to Samarkand and Merv. Most tackled the Wakhan Corridor past the Hindu Kush to Balkh and thence on to Merv. From Merv traders travelled to Constantinople through Syria, stopping off at Baghdad on the way. A few made for Damascus or Antioch.

Trade along the Silk Road continued until the second century AD when the Han Dynasty lost its grip on the Tarim Basin Kingdoms, while in Persia rulers changed and relatively safe passage for the traders was lost. Sea routes became better used as maritime technology was refined, and the southern

Silk Road was replaced by a northern route through the Heavenly Mountains, a route dominated by the Sogdian people in the fifth and sixth centuries.

By the time of the Tang Dynasty (AD 618-907) the Silk Road had fallen into disuse. The Persians had acquired the knowledge of silk production and the more economic and less arduous sea routes to Guangzhou (Canton) were becoming more popular.

Western Travellers on the Silk Road

Marco Polo is probably the best known and earliest traveller from Europe to the Orient and it was along the Silk Road in the 1270s that he first travelled the route. His father and uncle made the trip first and Marco followed from Venice. After four years (the journey is described in his classic book *Travels*) he arrived in Peking at the court of Kublai Khan.

Following in Marco Polo's footsteps were many travellers, the most famous being Benedict de Goes in the 16th century; Sven Hedin and Sir Aurel Stein, in the late nineteenth century and Albert von Le Coq and Paul Pelliot in the early part of the twentieth century. It was in the 1870s that a German, Ferdinand von Richthofen, named the route 'Silk Road'.

Travelling the Silk Road Today

The Road today is a comfortable and beautiful way into the Middle Kingdom, leading straight to its most remote and fascinating province, Sinkiang. What used to be a scree path a few feet wide, clinging to a precipice with bridges often no more than a rope to be taken hand-over-hand, is now the superb Karakorum Highway. It is possible to take luxury tours, such as those listed below, in air-conditioned comfort through this savage and beautiful landscape. Rougher but rewarding tours are organised by the Pakistan Government Sponsored Pakistan Tours Limited, which take a week to reach Kashgar and back from Rawalpindi, or two weeks to Urumqi and back. There are many excellent companies providing rather more exciting itineraries which most firms will happily vary on request. Not that tours are necessary. For the more adventurous, the highway is open from 1st May to 30th October and you need nothing more than the right visas. Any private car can make it (past signs alternately announcing 'Slides Area — Drive Carefully and Relax — Slides Area Over') all the way to the Chinese checkpoint. As yet they cannot go further. But local buses cross once a day and connect with Chinese buses down to Uighur oasis. Bicycles and motorbikes make the crossing — even camels can be arranged. In fact only pedstrians are completely banned. Most of the villages on the Pakistani side have modest and sometimes charming hotels, which may convert you to the diet of apricots that is reputed to make the local Hunzakot tribesmen the longest-lived people on earth. On the Chinese side, accommodation and food will leave more to be

In the shadow of the Big Goose Pagoda (Da Tan Ta) Xi'an. This pagoda was built in 652 by the Emperor Gaozong for the Buddhist traveller Xuan Zang.

desired. As always, the advantage of travelling independently is the freedom to watch the vast landscapes without any sense of urgency. But it is time-consuming too, since travel conditions in this new, remote country are not always ideal. The happy medium is probably a privately tailored tour by a local company.

You should start in Islamabad, Pakistan's modern capital set in the gentle foothills of the Himalayas. There are now excellent international flight connections to Islamabad, and, indeed, if your budget allows, you can fly the first leg of the journey proper to Gilgit. This is a hair-raising and spectacular trip, as the little 'plane weaves through mountains which are higher than its own flying ceiling. Understandably, flights only leave when conditions are perfect, so, although in principle it takes less than an hour it may take several days to reach Gilgit. The road starts along a more gentle route, crossing the Potwar plateau, past the ruins of Taxila, an ancient city visited by Alexander the Great, Ashoka, and finally, Attila.

At Gilgit, a centre for Chinese silks, the road begins to climb in earnest, though almost imperceptibly, such is the quality of the engineering. It reaches Hunza, the original Shangri-La, after sixty miles. Here Spring is an unexpected blur of colour against the gigantic face of Rakapochi: thousands of apricots blossom, and there are rosebushes the size of trees. Then the valley begins to close in. The crags and pinnacles gradually encroach on the road until the Khunjerab Pass, where the long descent to Kashgar begins. There, like Marco Polo, you can relish ice-cream where it was invented, on the edge of the Gobi.

To continue the journey along the Silk Road into China your easiest and probably most satisfying option is to join one of the many excellent tours. With minimum effort you will be guided along the road, stopping at the ancient trading posts from Kashgar to Xi'an. Many of the tours allow you the freedom to make your own adjustments, but most last about four weeks and, as the road is closed in winter, they only operate between May and September. You can also travel the Silk Road from Xi'an taking flights or travelling by train to Lanzhou and Dunhuang. The train journey obviously takes longer but the view of the Jiayuguan fort makes the trip worthwhile. A combination of bus and train or 'plane if you have limited time can take you to all the oasis towns as far as Kashgar. The situation in China at the present time makes it imperative to consult The Chinese Travel Service or local Chinese Embassy to keep up to date with travel arrangements and possibilities which are changing all the time.

A golden Buddha in Big Goose Pagoda. Here Buddhist Sanskrit manuscripts were translated into Chinese by Xuan Zang.

Big Goose Pagoda contains
many splendid carved Buddhas
and a history of Xuan Zang.

Background Information

China is the largest country in the world after the USSR and Canada, it covers an area of 9.6 million sq. km. China holds 22 per cent of the world's population, nearly one quarter of humanity at almost 1.1bn. Fifty-six nationalities live in China, but the overwhelming majority (93-94 per cent) of the population is ethnic Chinese, known as the Han nationality. The remaining percentage are minority nationalities such as Tibetan, Mongolian, Uighur, Korean and Miao.

Climate

Owing to China's enormous size, covering forty-nine degrees latitude from north to south, there are major climatic variations within the country from subarctic to tropical. The north-east experiences hot and dry summers from 21°C (70°F) to 26°C (79°F) with very cold winters from −17°C (2°F) to −7°C (21°F); the north and centre of the country have hot summers from 21°C (70°F) to 32°C (90°F) and cold winters from −10°C (14°F) to −2°C (28°F); the south-east region has a high rainfall with semi tropical summers from 23°C (73°F) to 32°C (90°F) and cool winters from 0°C (32°F) to 8°C (47°F).

The climate on the Silk Road itself varies greatly from the region's seasonal averages to searing desert heat in the summer and freezing temperatures in the mountains in winter. The oasis towns have a rather more Mediterranean climate.

Avoid high summer, Xi'an can reach temperatures approaching 100°F (38°C) and Turfan even higher. Travel in spring or autumn.

Language

Among the enormous number of local Chinese dialects, Mandarin is the most widely spoken. Written Chinese has no alphabet, but is made up of thousands of 'word pictures' called characters.

English is spoken in places which deal regularly with foreigners, such as hotels and friendly stores, but not widely spoken by the population in general.

Information sources

Many foreign newspapers and magazines are available at hotel lobbies and foreign bookstores, e.g. *Time, Newsweek, Asian Wall Street Journal, London Times, The New York Times*. Chinese daily publications appear such as the *China Daily*.

Health

Hospital services are excellent and medical costs are low. Many traditional forms of medicine are still used, but it is advisable to bring some standard western medicines for cold and stomach troubles.

All water should be regarded as being potentially contaminated. Drinking tap water anywhere in China is inadvisable. All hotels provide thermos of hot boiled water and a carafe of cold boiled water in every room. Mineral water can be bought in shops and restaurants.

Tipping

Many hotels and restaurants levy a 10 per cent service charge. Elsewhere, it is not customary to tip; the authorities disapprove of the practice as it is considered insulting and may cause embarrassment. Often the best gift for an official guide is a western reference book on China.

Currency

Chinese currency is called 'Renminbi'. It is denominated into yuan, jiao and fen. Special currency is issued for visitors, printed 'foreign exchange certificate' on the reverse. Neither currency can be purchased outside China, except in the form of traveller's cheques issued by the Bank of China.

Electricity

Throughout China the voltage is 220v, 50 cycles. It has no standard outlet. Some hotels will provide plugs.

Dress

In general, dress in China is fairly informal. Comfortable shoes are a must, as sightseeing in China involves a lot of walking and climbing. Women in China still dress quite conservatively and do not wear much make-up or jewellery.

Shopping

Tourists are inevitably taken to Friendly Stores, Youyi Shangdian, which are found in every city. These stores offer a wide variety of Chinese export wares as well as imported products. Only foreign Exchange Certificates are accepted at these stores and at hotels.

National Holidays

Chinese work 48 hours a week with Sunday as a rest day. The main holidays are:

New Years Day   January 1

Spring Festival   3 Day holiday in either January or February

International Labour Day   May 1

Chinese National Day   October 1

The Great Mosque Xi'an. Built in the 1300s the Mosque comprises a series of halls and courtyards. It is the focus for the large Muslim population of Xi'an who worship there daily.

ABOVE **The Great Mosque is decidedly Chinese in character, designed to cultivate a placid and tranquil atmosphere for prayer.**
FAR RIGHT **Twenty miles east of Xi'an are the Huaqing Springs. For nearly 3000 years the Chinese have visited this resort. Most of the buildings seen today date from only the turn of this century.**

Hours of Business

Shops: Open daily from 9am-9pm.
Banks: Currency can be exchanged at banking counters in hotels and stores. There are no standard hours of business for the exchange counters in hotels.

Communications

Telephones: Local intracity calls are free. International calls are priced according to destination and time, the clarity of sound varying enormously. The deluxe hotels offer direct-dialling facilities. Others must be booked in advance, and sometimes documentation filled out.
Post: All leading hotels have a post bureau or centre providing services. Incoming mail to China takes at least two and sometimes as much as three weeks.
Telex, Telegram, Fax: These can be sent from the deluxe hotels or from the post office. Telegrams are charged by the word, Fax and Telex by the minute.

Travel and Tours

Foreign tour groups wishing to travel to China may contact direct a local travel agency to join a full package tour arranged by a tour operator or get in touch with the Chinese Embassy or any association having business relations with China.
China International Travel Service (CITS) is the largest national tourist enterprise in China. With its head office in Beijing, CITS has branches in over 100 major cities and many overseas offices. All offer services to foreign tourists who wish to visit China or who are already in China.

Transportation

Air: The most practical means of travel between cities. The network is operated by the Civil Aviation Administration of China (CAAC). It covers over 166 routes, connecting more than 80 cities. Tickets can be purchased at CITS or direct from the CAAC offices in China. Make reservations well in advance.
Train: These are almost as expensive as plane fares (on average only 25 per cent cheaper). The classes consist of soft seat, soft sleeper, dining car, hard seat and hard sleeper. Although punctual, the trains are slow. It is advisable to book in advance.
Car and Taxi: Foreigners are not allowed to drive in China. There are no self-drive facilities, but all the superior hotels can arrange chauffered cars. It is advisable to provide destinations written in Chinese, as drivers do not usually speak English.
Buses: These are cheap but are often overcrowded, hot and slow. Not recommended as communication problems may arise with the driver when locating the bus stop.

Tourist information centres

Beijing: 6 East Chang'an Avenue, Beijing (512 1122)

Hong Kong: Unit 601, 6th Floor, Tower 11, South Seas Centre, 75 Mody Road, Tsim Sha Tsui East, Kowloon, Hong Kong (721 5317)

Tokyo: 6F Hanchidai Hamamatsu-cho, Minato-ku, Tokyo (433 1461)

London: 4 Glentworth Street, London (935 9427)

New York: Lincoln Building, 60 East 42nd Street, Suite 465, New York (867 0271)

Paris: 51 Rue Ste-Anne, 75002 Paris (42 96 95 48)

Frankfurt: Eschenheimer Anlage 28, D-6000 Frankfurt am Main-1 (555292)

Sydney: 33/336 Sussex Street, Sydney (276 9674)

Further reading

BEHIND THE WALL by Colin Thubron

INTO CHINA by John Lowe

THE CHINA GUIDEBOOK

THE LONG MARCH by Anthony Lawrence

FODOR'S 89 GUIDE

INDEX

ACKNOWLEDGEMENTS

Captions: *Caroline Ballinger*

Travelling the Silk Road: *Alexander Fyjis-Walker, Georgina Arbuthnott and Bernadine McGinty*

Special thanks to *Willie Landels*

Commissioning Editor: *Trevor Dolby*
Art Director: *Alyson Kyles with Peter Bridgewater Design*
Design Assistants: *Sarah Nunan, Sarah Pollock*
Production: *Janet Slater*
Typesetting: *Litho Link Ltd.*
Text set in Akzidenz Grotesque light.